Grasshoppers and Crickets

By Theresa Greenaway
Photography by Chris Fairclough

RSVP

**RAINTREE
STECK-VAUGHN**
PUBLISHERS
A Steck-Vaughn Company

Austin, Texas

Published by Raintree Steck-Vaughn Publishers, an imprint of Steck-Vaughn Company.

Acknowledgments
Project Editors: Gianna Williams, Kathy DeVico
Project Manager: Joyce Spicer
Illustrators: Tim Hayward and Stefan Chabluk
Design: Ian Winton

Planned and produced by Discovery Books

Library of Congress Cataloging-in-Publication Data
Greenaway, Theresa, 1947–
Grasshoppers and crickets/by Theresa Greenaway; photography by Chris Fairclough.
p. cm. — (Minipets)
Includes bibliographical references (p. 30) and index.
Summary: Provides information on the identification, life cycle, and habitats of grasshoppers, crickets, and katydids, as well as on how to collect and care for them as pets.
ISBN 0-8172-5590-7
1. Grasshoppers as pets — Juvenile literature. 2. Crickets as pets — Juvenile literature. 3. Grasshoppers — Juvenile literature. 4. Crickets — Juvenile literature. 5. Katydids as pets — Juvenile literature. 6. Katydids — Juvenile literature. [1. Grasshoppers as pets. 2. Crickets as pets. 3. Katydids as pets. 4. Grasshoppers. 5. Crickets. 6. Katydids. 7. Pets.] I. Fairclough, Chris, ill. II. Title. III. Series: Greenaway, Theresa, 1947–   Minipets.
SF459.G7G74   1999
638' . 5726—dc21   98-34085
CIP   AC
1 2 3 4 5 6 7 8 9 0 LB 02 01 00 99
Printed and bound in the United States of America.

Words explained in the glossary appear in **bold** the first time they are used in the text.

> ## WARNING
> Many crickets can bite—hard!

Contents

Keeping Grasshoppers and Crickets

Have you ever thought about keeping grasshoppers, crickets, or **katydids** as pets? There are about 20,000 kinds, or species, of crickets and grasshoppers in the world today.

Burrowing cricket

Mole crickets are odd-shaped brown crickets that burrow underground. They dig with their front legs, which are like big, clawed **spades**. The bodies of many kinds are covered with fine hairs.

If you walk through long grass on a warm day, you can see grasshoppers leaping in all directions. They blend in so well with their background, it is quite hard to spot them until they jump.

The singing noise made by crickets and grasshoppers lets us know that summer has arrived. Their high-pitched sounds tell other crickets and grasshoppers where they are located.

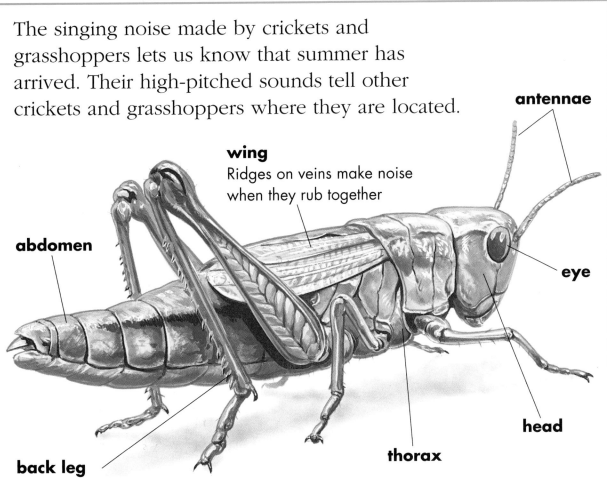

antennae

wing
Ridges on veins make noise when they rub together

abdomen

eye

head

thorax

back leg
Toothlike ridges to make chirping sound

Grasshoppers and crickets hatch from tiny eggs. The hatchlings, or **nymphs**, look like little adults without wings. They eat and eat. As the nymphs grow, they **molt**. After every molt, they are a little larger and a bit more adultlike.

The nymphs molt four or five times. After the final molt, they are fully grown. Many of them have large wings. Some have even changed color. They are ready to search for a mate.

Finding Grasshoppers and Crickets

Most crickets and grasshoppers live in grasslands, deserts, and forests. It is often much easier to hear a grasshopper or cricket than it is to see one! Some crickets and grasshoppers "sing" on hot, sunny days. Others prefer evenings and warm nights.

Grasshoppers, crickets, and katydids are hard to see because they often blend in with their background. Then, if they keep still, a hungry enemy might not see them. Crickets and katydids can often be found on trees and bushes, hiding among the leaves. It is hard to spot a bright green cricket sitting on a bright green leaf!

Katydids often have front wings that look like living or dead leaves. Grasshoppers can be found on a variety of plants. But a grassy field is a good place to start looking and listening.

▲ Can you spot the katydid hiding among these leaves? It is perfectly camouflaged to match its surroundings.

Singing hoppers

Grasshoppers and **locusts** make their song by rubbing the toothed, inside edges of their long, back legs over the hardened veins of their front wings. Crickets and katydids sing by rubbing a ridged edge of a front wing against a hardened area on a back wing.

Some crickets live under rocks and stones, and others live in the soil or in caves. These crickets are mostly dull brown in color. Try searching for them in **leaf litter** and in rocky places.

Grasshoppers and crickets leap all over the place when they are disturbed, so they are very hard to catch!

Jumping Jiminy!

Grasshoppers and many crickets have powerful muscles in their back legs. These enable them to jump again and again without growing tired. The most athletic grasshoppers can jump distances of up to 10 feet (3 m)!

Try holding a jar in one hand and a lid in the other. Move the jar slowly toward the grasshopper in one direction, and the lid slowly toward it in the other. If you are lucky, the insect will leap straight into the jar, and you can quickly put the lid on it.

Another way to catch these insects is to use
a net. Slowly sweep the net through the long
grass. Keep trying. With practice you will start
to catch these jumping insects.

Put your catches into jars or plastic containers,
and replace the lids quickly so that they do not
escape. Make sure that there are airholes in the
lids. Handle your new pets carefully. If you hold
them by a leg, they will shed it and escape.

Identifying Your Minipets

Now that you have a collection of hoppers, it is time to find out what they are. You will need an illustrated book about the crickets, katydids, and grasshoppers in your area, and a hand lens to see the insects clearly. Keep a notebook and pencil beside you. When you have identified one of your pets, write down its name.

To find out whether you have crickets, katydids, or grasshoppers, look carefully at their feelers. Crickets and katydids have long, thin feelers that may be longer than their bodies. Grasshoppers have short feelers that are much thicker than those of crickets.

Note the color and size of your pets, and whether they are slim or wide. Remember that young insects will be much smaller than adults. Look at the shape of the folded wings. Some look long and thin, while others look broad.

Make a note of any unusual features, such as a bad smell. These are clues that will help with your identification. Avoid touching larger insects with your fingers, because some of them bite quite hard.

Painted grasshopper

Painted grasshoppers are found in the deserts of the southwestern United States and Mexico. They protect themselves from **predators** by tasting terrible! Their brightly colored bodies are a warning to beware.

Providing a Home

To make homes for your pets, you will need some large jars or aquariums. The insects that you collected in grassy places will need a layer of soil in the bottom of their container.

Plant tufts of grass and other small plants that your hoppers were eating when you found them. Make sure the soil is damp enough for the plants to survive.

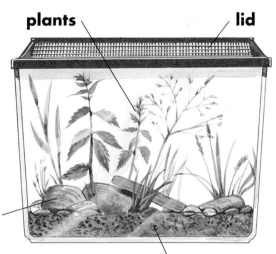

plants **lid**

stones

damp soil

For insects that you found on bushes, stand some cut twigs in a jar of water in their container. Crickets that live on the ground need dark places to hide. Put a thick layer of leaf litter with pieces of bark and flat stones at the base of their container.

If your aquarium doesn't have a lid, you can make one from fine wire mesh or net material. Make a "sleeve" of netting at one corner. Tie it with a piece of string so that nothing can crawl out. You can use this later to put food into the container without letting the insects escape.

Desert cricket

By day, the dune cricket stays in an underground burrow in the hot, dry Namib Desert. It only comes out at night, when the air is cooler. The dune cricket's hind feet are flat lobes fringed with hairs. They keep it from sinking into the sand.

Grasshopper and Cricket Care

When you collect grasshoppers and crickets, note where you found them. If they were feeding on a plant, take a piece of it back to identify. Many crickets are **carnivores**. Unless you can identify them, you will not know if they eat other insects or just plants.

Some katydids and crickets will eat almost anything—even their dead brothers and sisters! Some types of grasshoppers are crop pests.

If your pet does not seem to be eating, try offering it a variety of different foods. Put some **aphids** and other small bugs into its container, and watch carefully to see what happens. Try giving it oat flakes, crusts of bread, or small pieces of apples, cucumbers, or tomatoes.

Most insects need to drink, so put a lid filled with water into each container. Be sure to change the water every day.

Ears everywhere!

The ears of grasshoppers and crickets are not on their heads. Grasshoppers have ears on their stomachs, hidden by their wings. Locusts and katydids have ears above their hind legs (below).

Although many grasshoppers enjoy warm sunshine, they do not like to be too hot. So do not leave your minipets in the sun, or they will die.

See How They Grow

If you look closely at your crickets, katydids, and grasshoppers, you will notice that they have tough outer coats, or exoskeletons. These protect the insects from damage. Insects do not have bones. Instead, their muscles are attached to the inside of their exoskeletons. This allows the insects to move about.

A grasshopper or cricket's exoskeleton does not stretch or grow. So, after a while, a young insect has to molt.

Watch carefully if you think one of your grasshoppers or crickets is about to molt. The old coat splits near the head, and the insect struggles to release its head, feelers, and front legs. Then it wiggles the rest of its body free.

Sharp eyesight

Grasshoppers, katydids, and most crickets have large eyes that can detect even the slightest movements. They can also tell when it is getting lighter or darker.

◀ This longhorn grasshopper from Central America is almost free of its molted skin.

For a short while, the new skin is soft so that it can stretch. But a soft insect is easy **prey**, and a newly molted hopper cannot jump out of harm's way.

If molting takes too long, the new skin will have hardened before the insect has time to wiggle its legs free. If a young grasshopper loses a leg, it doesn't matter too much. The leg grows back a little bit each time it molts.

Grasshopper and Cricket Enemies

Although many grasshoppers and crickets can jump or fly to escape from danger, they are still eaten by all kinds of creatures. During the day, they are hunted by birds, lizards, and foxes.

At night, bats and owls are their main enemies. These flying hunters hear the crickets singing, so they can find them in the dark.

Other insects, such as ants, also eat crickets and grasshoppers, and spiders trap them in their webs.

▲ A locust makes a tasty meal for this gecko lizard.

Cats, foxes, and young dogs pounce on crickets and grasshoppers, then eat them from under their paws. In tropical rain forests, monkeys search for them to eat high up in the treetops.

Which creatures do you think might try to catch grasshoppers and crickets in your area? Watch a cat catching grasshoppers. How often is the cat successful, and how many times does the insect manage to escape?

Startle display

The leaf katydid looks just like a dead leaf when at rest. But if it is disturbed, it spreads open its wings to reveal large, false eyespots. This startles predators, such as birds, long enough for the katydid to escape.

Multiplication

Like all other insects, grasshoppers and crickets have to pair up before they can produce eggs. If your pets are males and females of the same kind, you can watch them courting.

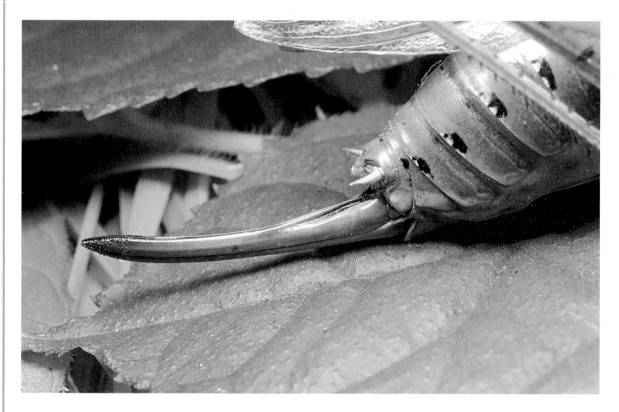

Grasshoppers and crickets sing to let any likely mates know that they are close by. Each kind of singing cricket, grasshopper, or katydid has its own special call. Can you tell the difference between them?

▲ Female crickets and katydids lay their eggs with a long, thin organ called an ovipositor.

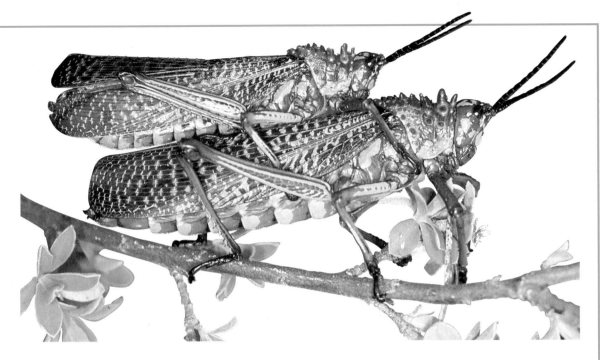

▲ These brightly colored grasshoppers are from the tropical forests of Madagascar.

Laying eggs

When the female grasshopper is ready to lay her eggs, she pushes the tip of her abdomen into the ground. Then she squeezes out the eggs. She squirts out a bubbly liquid that sets into a tough egg case.

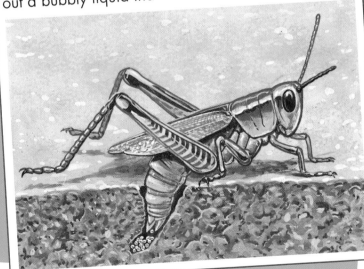

Some grasshoppers, especially those that live in tropical rain forests, are brightly colored. They flash their wings and move their beautifully patterned bodies to attract mates. But some male katydids will fight over females if they meet.

When Winter Comes

Grasshoppers and crickets cannot survive the cold, so they die when winter comes. Some crickets escape the cold by living inside houses. But most adults die after they have laid their eggs and when the cold weather arrives.

Protected from the frosts, the eggs will survive the winter months to hatch in the spring.

▼ Under the ground, cricket and grasshopper eggs will survive the harsh winter.

In tropical countries, grasshoppers and crickets may lay their eggs at the beginning of the dry season. This is a difficult time for insects and other animals. The plants lose their leaves and die, so there is little to eat. The eggs will only hatch when the rains return and the plants grow once more.

Your pets may have laid eggs in their containers before they died. Just in case, put the container outside. Make sure it is sheltered from rain. When spring comes, put the container in the sunshine. But make sure it does not get too hot. Also be sure that the soil in the container is damp.

Cooloola monster

In 1976 a new kind of cricket was discovered in Queensland, Australia. Its appearance is so strange that it was called the cooloola monster. It lives underground. Only the males come to the surface after rain at night.

Keeping a Record

Although scientists know a lot about grasshoppers and crickets, there is still plenty they do not know. If you take careful notes about your katydids, crickets, and grasshoppers, your notebook will become an interesting and valuable record of your minipets.

Try making a scrapbook as well. Collect pictures and articles from magazines, and paste them into it. If you really like grasshoppers and crickets, you might become an expert. You might even discover something that no one has found out before.

Grasshopper
Found: In the park
Date: August 28

My grasshopper has short antennae. Its wings are as long as its body.

OAK BUSH CRICKET

This cricket looks like a leaf.

cricket's ear

foreleg

I found this in a magazine.

Find out if there is a wildlife club for children in your area that you can join. Then, if you need help identifying your pets, there will be adults to help you.

You will also be able to talk about your pets with other children. Maybe you can show them how to catch and keep grasshoppers and crickets.

Swarming grasshoppers

The largest recorded grasshopper swarm was in 1949, in Oregon and California. All the plants over a 3,000-square mile (7,800-sq km) area were eaten.

You can find out more from books, CD-ROM encyclopedias, and the Internet. Reading about your grasshopper minipets is important. But so is seeing for yourself how they eat, molt, and behave.

Letting Them Go

As long as you look after them well, you can keep your grasshoppers, katydids, and crickets all summer. Most of them will die after they have laid their eggs. But some crickets will live much longer. Crickets that survive the winter live in sheltered places where they search for remains of food.

However long you decide to keep your pets, you must eventually return them to wherever you found them. Choose a dry morning for the species that are active during the day. For the kinds that are active by night, choose a dry evening. Release them in a sheltered spot, so that they can quickly hide from predators.

House crickets were once very common in kitchens. They lived beside kitchen stoves and under cupboards, feeding on scraps of fallen food.

Today these small, brown crickets are not often found in houses. Central heating has made most houses too dry for them.

▲ A house cricket jumps to safety in front of an open fire.

Giant weta

The fat, wingless giant weta from New Zealand weighs 2.5 ounces (70 g). If threatened by a predator, it sticks its spiny legs straight up into the air for defense.

Amazing Facts

This slow-moving Australian katydid lifts its wings to reveal a brilliant red, black, and blue body.

The male mole cricket builds the entrance to his burrow so that it acts as an **amplifier**. On a still evening, his song is heard up to 1.2 miles (2 km) away!

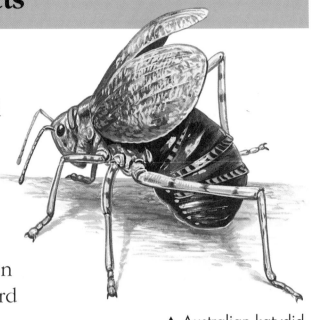

▲ Australian katydid

The Bible features plagues of desert locusts that ate crops and brought famine. A big swarm may contain as many as 50 billion insects! The damage done to crops even today is tremendous.

◄ Not only is this Amazonian katydid armed with scary spikes, but it also has powerful jaws that can really bite!

Not all deserts are sandy. The Namaqualand Desert in South Africa is rocky and pebbly. Some crickets look so much like pebbles that it is impossible to spot them until they move.

▼ Toothpick grasshopper

One type of cricket in the southeastern United States guards her eggs in a large, underground burrow. When the eggs hatch, she lays smaller eggs for the nymphs to eat.

The lubber grasshopper of North America has a messy way of protecting itself. When it is threatened, a smelly froth bubbles out of its sides. This keeps most enemies from touching or eating it.

The amazingly thin toothpick grasshopper looks just like a slender twig or grass stem. But look carefully, and you will see an eye and its long back jumping legs.

Further Reading

Coleman, Graham, and Tony Gibbons. *Grasshoppers*
  (Creepy Crawly series). Gareth Stevens, 1997.

Gerholdt, James E. *Grasshoppers* (Incredible Insects series).
  Abdo & Daughters, 1996.

Ross, Michael E. *Cricketology*. Lerner, 1996.

Ryden, Hope. *ABC of Crawlers and Flyers*. Clarion, 1996.

Glossary

Amplifier Something that makes noises sound louder.

Aphid A small, soft bug that sucks sap from the leaves and buds of plants.

Carnivore An animal that eats other living animals.

Katydid A large, green grasshopper with long antennae and long back legs.

Leaf litter A layer of fallen leaves, mostly from trees.

Locust A grasshopper that travels in swarms and strips areas of vegetation.

Molt To shed the tough outer coat, or exoskeleton.

Nymphs The young of an insect.

Predator An animal that hunts another animal for food.

Prey An animal that is hunted by another animal for food.

Spade A tool with a narrow, flat metal blade used for digging.

Index

The publishers would like to thank the following for their permission to reproduce photographs:
cover (grasshopper) © David Curl/Oxford Scientific Films, 4 John Cooke/Oxford Scientific Films, 7 top Michael
Fogden/Oxford Scientific Films, 7 bottom Kim Taylor/Bruce Coleman, 8 J. Brackenbury/Bruce Coleman, 11 Claude
Steelman/Oxford Scientific Films, 13 Michael Fogden/Oxford Scientific Films, 15 Jane Burton/Bruce Coleman, 16 Paul
Freed/Oxford Scientific Films, 17 Waina Cheng Ward/Bruce Coleman, 18 E. & D. Hosking/Frank Lane Picture Agency, 19
Michael Fogden/Oxford Scientific Films, 20 David G. Fox/Oxford Scientific Films, 21 Panda/E. Coppola/Frank Lane Picture
Agency, 22 L. West/Frank Lane Picture Agency, 23 Densey Clyne/Oxford Scientific Films, 27 top Kim Taylor/Bruce Coleman,
27 bottom Geoff Moon/Frank Lane Picure Agency, 28 M. P. L. Fogden/Bruce Coleman, 29 Michael Fogden/Bruce Coleman